ʃ[(

Unless noted all p.

Fireweed (*Epilobium angustifolium*)
This zines namesake

Most famous for its pioneer stature after a forest burn, a field of Fireweed is a glorious sight. I was initially attracted to this plant because of its hot pink flowers and its affinity to spring up in burnt out land-whether due to natural or civilization-made causes. It is eaten as a wild food, used as cordage & fire-starting tinder and notably as a medicinal herb. The leaves impress astringency and are virtuous for times when you need some: diarrhea, ulcers, minor wounds, & heavy menses.

Epilobium angustifolium L.

Fire-weed. Great or Spiked Willow-herb.

*Epilobium angustifolium* L. Sp. Pl. 347. 1753.
*C. angustifolium* Scop. Fl. Carn. Ed. 2, 1: 271. 1772.
*Epilobium spicatum* Lam. Fl. Fr. 3: 482. 1778.

Erect, rather stout, simple or branched, glabrous or often finely pubescent above, 2°–8° high. Leaves alternate, very short-petioled, lanceolate, entire or denticulate, 2′–6′ long, 4″–12″ wide, pale beneath, acute at the apex, narrowed at the base, thin, the lateral veins confluent in marginal loops; flowers 8″–15″ broad, purple, or sometimes white, in elongated terminal spike-like racemes; bracts mostly shorter than the pedicels; petals entire; style pubescent at the base; stigma 4-lobed; capsules 2′–3′ long, about 1½″ thick, finely canescent, at least when young; seeds about ½″ long, smooth, or nearly so, the coma long, whitish.

In dry soil, Greenland to Alaska, North Carolina, Indiana, Kansas; the Rocky Mountains to Arizona; Pacific Coast to California. Europe and Asia. Often abundant after forest fires. French-, bay- or Persian-willow. Rose-bay. Fire-top. Burnt weed. Purple rocket. French or bay willow-herb. Indian

http://www.swsbm.com/Britton-Brown/Epilobium_angustifolium.gif

## ※ Fireweed Syrup ※

An easy to take medicine for a little one down with diarrhea. This is an adaptation of a syrup recipe found in the excellent book Backyard Medicine by Julie Bruton-Seal and Matthew Seal.

Collect the fresh flowering heads and cover with water. Bring to a gentle simmer for about 5-10 minutes. Strain out herb using cheesecloth, a tea strainer or your hand. Measure the remaining liquid and add twice this measured amount in honey (1 cup liquid=2 cups honey)

Combine liquid and honey together in a pan. Add several squeezes of lemon or lime juice and add a *little* heat to make a uniform consistency. Allow to cool. Label a jar with ingredients and date and bottle the syrup. Store in the fridge. Give a teaspoon to kids and tablespoon to adults as needed.

## Childhood Friends
by Leah Wolfe

When I was a child, I lived on a threshold. The San Andreas fault divided the mountains bordering the high deserts of Southern California. Here plants from two ecosystems overlapped. The mountains in front of my house were a forest of Jeffrey Pines, Oaks, Huckleberries, and wildflowers. The lower hills behind my house were dotted with Joshua Trees, Scrub Oak, Sagebrush, Yerba Santa, and Prickly Poppies.

The plant I remember the most is Sagebrush. The way it smelled when I crushed it between my fingers. The extremely bitter taste. It was a comfort when my friends and I hid beneath its low branches at the edges of the playground.

Sagebrush is called *Artemisia tridentata*. It is not related to sage(*Salvia* species). Its relatives are Mugwort, Wormwood, Tarragon, and Southernwood. Many of the Artemisias are taken for purification both physically and spiritually. Most of them are taken as bitters to stimulate digestion through their actions on the gallbladder and liver.

Wormwood, historically taken as Absinthe, clears the doorway to the creativity. Absinthe was popular among artists and writers as a way to open the visionary mind. The drink earned a reputation as a poison, though it's unknown whether the constituent thujone or the colors and additives were to blame. The brilliant color of the spirit and its ability to give drinkers visions inspired the nickname "The Green Fairy."

Medicinally, it is often included in formulas to rid the digestive system of parasites. Wormwood is given to pigs as a natural vermifuge and anthelmintic; that is it stuns and expels parasitic worms. Externally as a poultice or ointment, it speeds the healing of inflammation in the joints or of the skin.

Another door opened by the Artemisias is to the dream world. Some place Mugwort above their beds to provoke lucid or vivid dreaming. The oil is rubbed on the forehead to stimulate the pineal gland, which secretes melatonin to promote deep sleep, creativity, and vision through the third eye. It is also used in the form of moxibustion to clear acupressure points by increasing circulation and reducing inflammation. It has a history of being used to purge parasites, as an emmenagogue (promote menstruation or purge the uterus), to calm hysteria and other nervous afflictions, and as a gallbladder/liver tonic.

My friend, Sagebrush, is often burned as a smudge to clear the air, chase away evil spirits, or transform dark energies. It is extremely bitter and its physical actions are similar to those of Mugwort and Wormwood. It helps me clear negative perspective so that I can see the best in people and the best in myself. I've had dreams of Sagebrush burning. The curling smoke lifts into my ancestry through bloodlines like rivers in a family tree. It clears space in my spirit for the good memories to surface and clears my lens of experience so that I can see anew.

**What plants call to you in your childhood memories?**

# 'Miranda's Magic Garden'

by Linda Atnip reviewed by Physick

Miranda is a lonely child in the middle of a large city. As no other children live nearby, she spends the majority of her time in the small garden behind her apartment building talking to the plants. One day, Miranda sighs and wishes that she could be a flower, at least then she would have other flowers as friends. To her astonishment the Sunflower answers, "We would like to be friends with you, too." Thus begins a magical journey for the young child. She is visited in her dreams by the Devas (Sunflower spirits) and an old woman named Keeper of the Earth, who grants Miranda the ability to see inside the invisible world of plants. In return she must grow a Magical Garden. The following night Miranda dreams that she is being chased by a Grizzly Bear in a thunderstorm. After she summons up the courage to turn around and confront her predator, the Bear shape-shifts into the Keeper of the Earth, who rewards her bravery with colorful magic seeds.

The next day, Miranda begins lovingly cultivating her own plot in the garden. She sings to the plants and cares for her new friends with great passion. Massive Sunflowers towered over the girl, while Hibiscus, Lilies, and Daisies surrounded her with a "living kaleidoscope of color."

Eventually, one of Miranda's neighbors takes a picture of her amazing garden and shows it to a newspaper reporter, who comes to interview the young gardener. When asked her secret to growing such tall Sunflowers, Miranda replies, "We grew the garden together. Plants know what they need to grow. If you listen to them with your inner ears, you can hear their voices. The flowers just want to be loved and cared for."

After the story ran, television crews and people from all over the city visited to witness the miraculous plot. Miranda then begins to teach other children as small gardens start to spring up throughout the city, and her wish for (human) friends finally comes true.

Children will feel empowered by a young female who is both strong and compassionate. Additionally, issues such as creative problem-solving are addresses when Miranda must deal with a Mole who is undoing all of her hard work. She creates a positive solution whereby she can remain friends with the Mole (and by extension all of her animal relations) and keep her garden plot. The soft illustrations, almost Waldorf-like in some cases, bring so much light to the pages that they almost appear to glow. Linda Atnip has crafted an inspirational story that children will never tire of reading. If they do however, not to worry because Linda has also made available an audio book version (which is great for children too young to read but who still hang on to every word of the story).

With so many remarkable books out there such as 'The Secret Life of Plants' by Tompkins and Bird, 'The Lost Language of Plants' by Stephen Harrod Buhner, and Derrick Jensen's 'A Language Older than Words,' it is wonderful to finally have a children's version.

******

Red clover

## Harvesting Wild Plants
by Jess

Spending a day wildcrafting is one of my favorite family activities. Using our senses to meet a plant where it is alive and growing deepens our understanding of its actions in the body. For me it is a personal and spiritual practice that no book or dried herb on the shelf can convey. However, many plants are diminishing in their wild populations due to greed & disconnection causing habitat destruction far and wide. For these reasons being a conscious earth-centered wildcrafter is of the up most importance.

+Learn what wild plants are endangered or threatened due to habitat loss or overharvesting in your bioregion. For example, popular herbs such as echinacea, black cohosh, slippery elm, wild yam, goldenseal and many more are at-risk in wild populations. United Plant Savers is a group with info on medicinal plant conservation that complies an at-risk list. Local plant groups are also helpful. If you buy herbs or herbal products inquire about how and where the herbs are harvested-do not purchase wild harvested endangered plants. Instead support people or farms that organically cultivate threatened plants. Find ethical medicine makers.

+Turn you yard into a medicinal and weedy herb sanctuary. Some say cultivated plants lack some of the spark of wild plants but nonetheless grow your own too. If you have woods try growing some of the more sensitive at-risk woodland plants. Con't...

+Get to know a piece of land for several seasons to a year **before** wild crafting. Is the herb I'd like to harvest plentiful and healthy, what will be my impact? Is it threatened or endangered? What animals and insects use this plant for shelter or food? Has there recently been or is there a predicted drought or other major weather event? Harvest when the specific plant parts are at their peak (i.e. the new leaves in spring).

+Make sure the area is free of pollutants such as electrical wires from above, pesticides, dog waste, old foundations & the road 50 yards or more. This can be a challenge in an urban place so do the best you can while minimizing your exposure.

+In addition to learning from an experienced wild crafter, **absolutely** positively ID a plant, if unsure don't harvest. If not more than 100% certain- don't do it! Nothing beats a wild-crafter, botanist or herbalist to help you learn plant I.D.'ing and respectful Earth care.

+Many herbalists ask the plants permission before harvesting it and leave an offering of thanks before leaving. The offering can be physical (strand of hair, tobacco) or a spoken blessing or prayer. Spend time sitting quietly with plants-they are good teachers.

+**Only** harvest as much plant that can be used and processed right away. It is easy to be overzealous but remember you may not be the only being using this plant. Start small.

+Above all have reverence for the land. Leave the area looking the same as it was when you arrived. Keep a wildcrafting log.

## Resources for More Information:

~~~~~~

*Books:*

Botany in a Day by Thomas Elpel

Making Plant Medicine by Richo Cech

The Forager's Harvest and Nature's Garden by Sam Thayer

*Internet:*

7Song
www.7song.com/files/Wildcrafting%20for%20the%20Practicing%20Herbalist.pdf

jim mcdonald
www.herbcraft.org/gathering.html

United Plant Savers
www.unitedplantsavers.org/

Howie Brounstein
www.botanicalstudies.net/wildcrafting/wildcrafting_beginners.php
~~~~~~

Kids from Magical Arts

Magical Arts ~~~~
With Dori Midnight

I have been teaching Magical Arts at an alternative public school in San Francisco for about 6 years. It began as a weekly class called Witchy Wednesdays, which quickly became so popular that we made a decision to offer it 2-3 days a week. It was offered for kindergarteners through 6th graders at Rooftop School, which is considered the most economically and ethnically diverse elementary school in the city.

Every class begins with a guided journey (we don't call them meditations because the kids get bored in meditations, but seem to love journeys) and a cup of tea. This is my secret to a calm classroom of 30 children: lemon balm, chamomile, rose petals, hibiscus, and mint tea. Personally, I think all schools should serve herbal tea to students and ramp up the chamomile when needed.

The class moves through the wheel of the year, helping kids to connect to the seasons through recipes, remedies, and craft projects. We make salves, teas, bath salts, syrups, and herbal treats, as well as magic wands, protective amulets, spirit guide stuffed animals, and the favorite class all year: magic potions. After a couple of classes in which kids learn to listen to herbs and stones using their "witch eyes and witch ears", we make a few essences of plants around the school yard. On Magic Potion day, the kids go on a guided meditation to understand what they might need some support with- maybe their parents aren't getting along, or they feel overwhelmed with jealousy, insecurity, or fears. Some kids make potions to help them see fairies or help make the world a better place. And some kids make secret love spell potions and blush when asked about them...Con't...

In a world in which kids are over-medicated and over-stimulated, taking time to go within, get quiet, and find resources in themselves and in nature is radical. Kids are hungry for magic and their imaginations allow them to be open to this kind of support from the invisible world. Encouraging kids to see the invisible and hear the silent language of plants undoes the spells of capitalism and scarcity that at times can lead us as adults into isolation and depression.

I like to think of Magical Arts class as a link from the present to the ancient- connecting kids with old traditions that make sense to them because it is our birthright. Kids learn about ancient healing arts, history, lore, and skills, giving them a sense of belonging in this world which is increasingly alienating. It's been amazing to see kids who are tracked in special ed classes during the day thrive and excel in Magical Arts class.

Diego, a 4th grader who is considered to be on the autistic spectrum, is one of the stars of the class. In the Stone Medicine class we did, Diego was deeply focused on holding the piece of rock to his ear and after 20 minutes told a circle of 25 kids that the stone told him its name and its healing properties: helping you feel at peace when things were loud and crazy all around you. Or one day Lucy, a 5th grader who has been totally into magical arts class since kindergarten, helped heal her sister's sting with calendula petals and a song.

These kids are not kids who would usually be exposed to such things; their parents are not herbalists, hippies, or witches. Most of them are supportive because they see how happy their kids are and how able they are to take care of themselves and each other.

One parent of a 2nd grader emailed me after school one day to tell me what her daughter said that night. There was some strife at home, but Addie was finding a lot of comfort in class. Here's her email:

Addie came home with this wand of plants today. She said,
*"I made this in Dori's class. The yarrow in it is for focus, lavender is peaceful, sage is healing. This magic that hangs here over us is my Protective Guide....I call it the Reef of the Goddess. Now I will say a blessing for it....*
*Oh, Reef of the Goddess. We believe in your magic. We bless you. We are blessed by you. When your petals fall down, we will refresh you. I am the bearer of my wand. Every person who visits me in my dreams comes from you, and every flower that comes down on me in the night will bless me as I sleep".*

I can't take credit for all that wisdom, but in class I continually witness the power of connecting kids to the magic that is already inside them. As people living on earth at such a critical time, when there is so much social injustice and environmental degradation, I feel certain that it is essential to healing our communities and planet that kids gain these kind of skills and wisdom.

"We believe in your magic"

## 'The Last Wild Witch'

### *An Eco-Fable for Kids and Other Free Spirits*

Written by Starhawk Illustrated by Lindy Kehoe
Reviewed by Physick

In the forest outside of a "perfect" town, where children line up in "perfect" lines and the day unfolds in "perfect" order, lives the last Wild Witch. She spends her days singing while making herbal soup for her animal neighbors who inhabit the woods around her cottage. Occasionally the breeze will carry the aroma into the town where the children, upon catching a whiff, become uncontrollable. A little taste of "wildness" inside them, they begin running, dancing, and laughing. The parents and city officials decide to put an end to this by attempting to drive out the last Wild Witch, first by clear-cutting the trees then by setting fire to the woods.

The children visit the Witch to seek guidance on how to stop the adults, but the Witch offers no advice - only sips of her herbal soup (which nourishes their inherent resolve and courage). When the adults return to level the forest, the children scatter into the woods and hide, preventing the fires from being lit. As they search about looking for the children, the adults realize how pleasant and therapeutic the wilderness is and upon meeting the last Wild Witch, realize that she reminds them of their grandmothers and is clearly no threat. The villagers decide that they need the forest and animals and agree to leave it as a protected area. And the last Wild Witch became a frequent visitor to the village, bringing her wildcrafted herbs and broth to ill residents.

Lindy Kehoe's enchanting illustrations compliment the storyline beautifully. A frequent contributor to We'Moon, Kehoe's flowing and intensely colorful artwork will capture the child's imagination. A marvelous book that would look right at home next to 'Shanleya's Quest' and 'I'm a Medicine Woman, Too' on your bookshelf.

# Earth Apple:

## The Bittersweet Medicine of Chamomile

By Kiva Rose

Do you REALLY know Chamomile?

Chamomile means "earth apple" which is easy to understand when we accidentally trample the flowers underfoot and suddenly smell the welcome fragrance of apples rising from the earth. In the same way, Spanish speaking peoples often use the name Manzanilla, literally meaning "little apple".

Even for those largely unfamiliar with herbs, the distinctive sweet scent of Chamomile is often both familiar and comforting. This plant is many people's first and perhaps only introduction to herbalism, often from a cup of honey-sweetened and belly-calming tea from their grandmother.

Many children enjoy eating the buds or just opened flowers, savoring the sweet aromatic taste of the plant, and rarely seeming to mind the slightly bitter aftertaste. Some patches of Chamomile, depending on phase of flowering and availability of moisture, are much more bitter than others but the fragrant sweetness persists even in the most bitter batches.

Far from irrelevant, these signature sensory characteristics of Chamomile that make the plant memorable in our minds are also the primary keys to understanding how to work with Matricaria as a medicine.

As with almost any herb, the taste and scent of Matricaria tells us a great deal about its properties, allowing us to use our senses to listen to the plant and understand its essence as a medicine. That blissfully apple-like scent that children so love to breathe in from the flowers tends to bring relaxed smiles to their faces and anyone who's ever drank a cup of the tea can testify to the relaxing, tension alleviating effects of the plant. Con't...

That aromatic component, stemming from the plant's high volatile oil content, is predictably nervine, meaning that it has a discernible effect on the nervous system. In this case, a specific relaxing, calming effect. Additionally, that same volatile oil content is responsible for Chamomile's actions as a carminative, relieving digestive stagnation in the form of gas, gut cramping and mild constipation. A traditional remedy by several North American indigenous tribes for the uterine cramps of girls just beginning their menstrual cycles, Chamomile is a mild relaxant for the smooth muscles of the gut, uterus, bladder and respiratory tract with a specific affinity for the gut.

Matricaria is not just aromatic, even in the sweetest Chamomile flowers we find a notably bitter aftertaste. Rather than ruining the flavor of an otherwise tasty herb, that bitter element enhances and expands the medicinal properties of the plant. The bitter flavor tells us that it has a distinct effect on the digestive system, even beyond the aromatic/carminative qualities.

The bitterness increases the secretion of digestive juices and enzymes in the gut, thereby improving digestion wherever there is a lack of secretions, which is a common cause of heartburn and many cases of general gut discomfort. This combined with its obvious nervine properties; Matricaria excels at treating what is commonly known as a "nervous stomach", which generally implies digestive upset concurrent with anxiety and nervous tension.

Volatile oils and bitter principles together make for a powerful ability to reduce inflammation and promote healing, especially in the gut. I rarely create a formula for those with leaky gut, irritable bowel syndrome or even Crohn's disease that doesn't contain some proportion of Chamomile.

Even as a simple, this pleasant tasting plant can very effectively reduce gut inflammation, pain and cramping while promoting healing of the mucosa and improving overall digestion. And of course, reducing any anxiety that may be aggravating or triggering the gut issues in the first place.

Just as it soothes and heals internally, Matricaria is also a first-rate external application for almost any case of inflammation, irritation, swelling and even potential infection. It finds its way into many of my compress formulas for eczema, psoriasis, atopic dermatitis and other common inflammatory skin conditions.

Steams, baths and infused oil are other effective ways of utilizing the calming, decongestive and healing properties of the herb. It's also the first plant I think of in addressing the discomfort, irritability, insomnia, belly upset and fever of teething in small children.

Chamomile is one of my favorite remedies for all sorts of eye inflammations and infections. It can be used as a warm compress or saline eyewash to reduce inflammation, possible infection and pain in the treatment of sties, conjunctivitis, pink eye and similar maladies.

It teams up especially well with any Rosa spp. petals where there is a great deal of redness, irritation and swelling in the eye and the surrounding area. Just be sure to strain all those tiny (and potentially irritating) bits of Chamomile flower before using as an eyewash.

Chamomile has a well-deserved reputation as an archetypal remedy for children (or as Matthew Wood says "children of any age"), especially where there is fussiness, restlessness, frequent digestive upset and a tendency to react strongly to any irritant or discomfort. Con't...

If one were to read the first dozen monograph on Matricaria they came across, the word "soothing" would be likely to show up in nearly every one. While now a somewhat clichéd representation of this common herb, it is nonetheless very accurate. There's a tendency by some of us to be less interested in the classic gentle herbs whose effects seem obvious, mild and less than profound. And yet, Chamomile has retained it's popularity and reputation over the years for a very a specific reason. It works. It's an effective, widely applicable, safe medicine well-loved by countless generations of mothers, herbalists and more recently, even medical doctors. This small but fragrant apple of the earth remains an invaluable medicine for all of us. Through both sweet and the bitter tastes, Chamomile provides us with a simple yet essential remedy.

**Considerations:** People with sensitivities to plants in the Aster family may have similar problems with Matricaria. Also note that Pineapple Weed (*M. discoidea*) often has a stronger bitter component and overall action than the common garden grown *M. recutita.*

**Common Name:** Chamomile, Manzanilla, Pineapple Weed

**Botanical Name:** *Matricaria recutita* (as well as *M. discoidea*) **Botanical Family:** Asteraceae

**Taste:** Aromatic, sweet, bitter

**Vital Actions:** relaxant nervine, relaxant diaphoretic, aromatic bitter/carminative, vulnerary

**Specific Indications:** Irritability, tension, heat, hypersensitivity to pain

**Energetics:** sl. Cool, dry

mullein

## Herbal Care for Everyone by Jess

In the U.S. we have a culture that values consumption, individualism, money, whiteness, disconnection from nature and gender binary. Partially as an alternative to the dominant culture I am very interested in making herbal knowledge & herbalists available to all. Herbal skills are often in the hands of folks who have the privilege and proximity to classes, books, teachers and places to grow or harvest plants. Given my interest in breaking down those barriers to care how can I also eat & pay bills & hold value to my work as community herbalist? As a parent I further realize the struggles of finding the adequate support needed to do all these things- not to mention that I benefit from all the privilege I was born into. How does one align their ideals and aspirations? Including our kids on this journey is important to sustaining momentum in community building.

Different herbalists have various approaches to keeping herbal work accessible. Herbal free clinics such as Ithaca Free Clinic in Ithaca, NY and Common Ground Health Clinic in New Orleans work to make clinical services available. Herb sharing circles are sometimes present in communities to exchange knowledge and valuable clinical skills all while helping people with their health needs. There may also be clinics that offer sliding scale or barter situations. Free schools, found in many larger cities, are an additional venue for spreading herbal knowledge. However wonderful they are some may not reach out of the community they sprang from and can have little effect on a diverse population. How are you working to be a rooted, accessible herbalist?

I have grappled with how to be truly available and stay balanced with my personal life. Although these thoughts are evolving currently I offer sliding scale and barter options for many classes & herbal goods. We can value our medicine makers, wildcrafters and support them with money (if you can, do more, less if not) or useful trades so that they can continue their good work. I'll happily exchange herbal medicines for veggies, meat or childcare. I try to let go of guilt for charging a fair price so that I can continue to teach and craft. I am completely open to a discussion on how to make it work. I am also honest about my experience level and love to partner with people to figure out their health needs-I certainly do not see myself as an expert and welcome the chance to share. Ideally I'd love to develop an herbal educator co-op where we all get are needs met-for food, friendship, community and health. As long as we organize child care...

Evening primrose

# Anywhere is Possible: An Interview with a Happy Feral Family
by Netoto

*The unfiltered, unpolluted air, the flicker of wild birds, real sunshine and rain, mud to be tasted and tree bark to grasp, the sounds of wind and water - all these are not vague and pleasant amenities for the infant, but the stuff out of which its second grounding, even while in its mother's arms, has begun. - Paul Shepard*

## What are some of your favorite aspects of traveling with your kids?

The best thing about traveling with my kids is time. In a homesteading environment or housey-house environment, or any urban to rural environment, there is always so much to do; there is building, milking, planting, cleaning, cooking, hobbies, etc. but when traveling and living in a wild environment, I feel like our time is our own, to do with whatever we want.

We do silent walks through the woods, tracking, listening, connecting, we do yoga for hours, we snuggle and read. We are somehow able to disconnect from the "entertain me" reality that is so prevalent among folks today and enter into a state of blissful being, where entertainment is unnecessary because all of living is deep and meaningful.

I feel like there is a false sense of security that living in a house on a block in a neighborhood fosters; or even land-based families where the family farm is the basis of all livelihood and security that is stifling and prevents development of deep imagination. When a person is tied to a piece of land so completely that it seems impossible to go anywhere else for more than a few weeks, that blanket of security actually becomes a net - a trap. The experience of being semi-nomadic with my children is teaching each of us that anything is possible; anywhere is possible. There are no boundaries, no "should's." There is simply the moment and in it we can be anything.

*Let me live where I will, on this side is the city, on that the wilderness, and ever I am leaving the city more and more, and withdrawing into the wilderness. - Henry David Thoreau*

## What are the kids favorite parts of traveling?

I think that one thing they love about travel is absolute freedom. In houses there is a sense of what one can and cannot do; but in the woods - in the wild, there is openness and expansion. When we have been in an urban environment, and first come back to the wild, I see in my kids an unfolding and release. Sloughing off the bullshit of a false reality. I see the light return to their eyes and see them truly begin again to enjoy; to experience the flow of deep joyful living. We also sing silly songs, a lot! One of us will start a story song, then pass it around and that's a lot of fun!

*In the woods, is perpetual youth. - Ralph Waldo Emerson*

## How do your kids experience herbal magick?

This is constantly under development. Myself, and the folks that I resonate with, are deeply connected with plant energy on many levels. So for the kids, their intro into this realm is deep and wide. We seek to connect with the biodiversity of each new realm that we inhabit, forming relationships with both plant and animal and seeking to know and utilize the medicines of each new place. So when we get to a new locale, we will do plant walks and begin to meet and sit with the plants there, to come into their presence; we will nibble, gather specimens, smell, touch and speak with these new friends. We use fields guides to key out what we don't know, then begin to utilize these things into our daily lives. I feel very strongly about the importance of wild foods in the diet, for well-being and as a way of deeply connecting with place.

So we go from the mundane (what is the best thing to wipe an ass with here?) through foods into medicines and utility. We make baskets and cordage, we play with plants, we make fire. All of this is magick. I am learning that magick is not an external act, but a deep internal state of being. When we are most fully present in our self, and most actively engaged in living and manifesting our vision and truth, then we step into the magician's realm and we participate with the magick that is the wild. Con't...

*We must take our children into the wild, introduce them to the plants, and teach them of their connection to the Earth. In instilling in our children a respect for plant medicine, we not only care for their tender bodies but help pass along the seeds of a tradition that is as old as human life itself.*
*- Rosemary Gladstar*

## Why do you feel it's important to introduce kids to wild foods and herbs?

We are wild beings that have been clothed in little suits and taught to walk to the beat of a controlled drum. We are the organ grinder's monkey, and rewilding is deeply seeking to shed this paradigm and reconnect with our deep biological roots, the ones that link us to this earth and to the sky and to all living things. When we eat domesticated food, we become more and more domesticated. Conversely, when we take in nourishment from the wild, we take in energy from our root, from the same biological base that has nourished us since the Pleistocene. We are still genetically the same animal we were then; we have been tamed - not completely domesticated. I feel like one of the most radical and revolutionary things folks can do right now is to eat something wild every day. To keep our connection to free beings (plant, animal, mountains) intact so that we can be free.

*But wild beings we still were, our sensations and ourselves still one, knowing that to pursue pleasure was life. All that was beautiful and pleasant we would reach for with our hands, our mouths, our ears, our eyes, every part of us, not in order to possess it, but in order to love it, to enjoy it, to be it. For our senses were our way of experiencing everything we wished by becoming whatever we sensed.*
*- Feral Faun*

## What kinds of struggles do you face and how can folks help traveling families?

I face many struggles. I face my families judgment, I face societies judgment, I struggle with fear of the law, money is an issue. I wonder if I am shortchanging my kids for not giving them the "normal" upbringing that society says they need. I struggle with not feeling secure because of lack of a "permanent" land base. I struggle with each of these things, weighing and measuring them, trying to speak my truth.

There are many ways that more sedentary people can support nomadic wild folks. Money is always an issue, as well as food support and tool donations, and simply being supportive and helping to undo the stereotypes that pervade the dominant culture. But perhaps the most important step that needs to develop is that folks with land need to be open to nomadic folks coming through. I envision a green corridor that weaves National forests and private land into a beautiful tapestry of sharing that would allow for people like us to travel from forest to farm, trading domestic goods for wild ones in a symbiotic relationship that allows for farm folks to have helping hands when they need it, and for nomadic folks to have welcome spaces. If these communities have dedicated spaces for nomadic travelers, then these nomadic folks really need to show up and help on the farm - no slackers; but beautiful mutuality and sharing.

*All types of projects, in the garden and in the community, benefit greatly from the inclusion of children. Children can contribute fresh ideas and comic relief and add new dimensions to any project. And while it is parents who choose to make children and care for them - or sadly, sometimes not - it is the responsibility of the entire community to create an environment that will encourage children to grow into happy, creative adults. - Heather C. Flores*

## How do you manage to cope with such a massive undertaking?

I cope with grace and patience because I recognize that for me, there is no alternative. My truth tells me that the current system is a farce and on the brink of collapse and that my personal revolution is to teach and live in such a way that the other options (like the dominant paradigm) don't compare. In other words, I am striving to live my life in such a way that folks who are paying attention to the signs around us respond with something like "Of course, that makes so much sense!" I tried for almost 10 years to fit into the norm and I almost went nuts. So a few years back I left my house, my husband and my reality and took a road trip out west with myself and my children and had a quiet revolution, from which I have not looked back. Con't...

I have continued on this journey into natural building, farming, herding, etc., to where if find myself now, which is on an Abbey-like path that leads ever more rocky and winding and wild, and sometimes lonely, but with the most amazing views! It is this feeling of rewilding, of being a catalyst of the sustainable evolution of our species that keeps me going. I am also deeply moved by Paul Shephard, Dale Pendell, Ed Abbey, Jesse Wolf Hardin, and a few other folks who encourage me on this path, not of rebellion but of re-evolution

*I devote myself to simplicity and returned to it all, left that workaday life for this wisdom of wandering, for this wildness of rivers-and-mountains clarity.*
*- Hseih Ling-yun*

## Is there a support network for nomadic mamas?

I have not found much support until very recently for nomadic mamas. I have found that most communities reject mothers with children on the premise that we cannot participate because we are always caring for our young, which is laughable in that we show up more than many! We are used to multi-tasking and mothering - the ability to nurture and care for those around us and I find that often this is the element most lacking in communities.

I am currently traveling with four mamas, two papas, two single adults, and nine kids. This is by far the most supportive and inspiring experience of having children thus far! We are forming rituals and routines around mealtimes, morning circles, etc. And we are finding solidarity in our decisions. The kids are learning not to play us against each other because we are finding unity in our decisions. Also, food seems to be the most challenging, as everyone wants things their way and we simply are not willing to cater to those many layered requests. So the cook decides what we eat, and that's what we eat. We are working to develop a solid ethos of eating and by providing all healthy choices many of the battles around food are falling away beautifully.

Also, by having many hands around to gather wood, haul water and prepare meals, I find that for the first time since I've had children, I actually have free time. This, to me, is one of the most exciting aspects of community living!

I would like to see this network expand into something that honors the roll of mother and father and child; to a place where it is understood that healthy vibrant communities include parents and children as well as young single adults. The people and places that I have experienced which embrace the family unit are more diverse and thriving and multi-dimensional than those who are simply seeking hands to work the farm.

*But caring for the baby was not the mother's job alone. Everyone looked after him. Men and women alike adore little children, and even the teenage boys from next door were not embarrassed to be seen cooing over little Angchuk or rocking him to sleep with a lullaby. - Helena Norberg-Hodge*

## How has the relationships between your children and the plant world blossomed?

The unfolding of the plant spirits to the children is so beautiful to witness. Recently I walked up on my 4 year old giving a mixed age group a talk about *Usnea* and its many uses and how to check for the thread to make sure it wasn't just "pretending" to be Usni! My heart swelled with such joy that he was giving this talk and felt confident enough in his understanding to share. This is one of many examples children being so ready to receive these sacred teachings. My 8 year old has been going on mushroom walks with one of our community and really beginning to learn about poly pores and the three things to watch out for. By being surrounded with folks who are building relationships with the plant realm, our children are learning to do so, and this to me, is one of the deepest lessons of this entire movement. Our children will repeat what they see. When I look around the reality of the dominant paradigm, I see a series of poor decisions being replicated by humans, creatures of habit. So by identifying and understanding this characteristic of our selves, we can begin very early in life to set healthy patterns and habits, knowing that these, too, will be replicated. This is the quiet revolution, the one that starts in ourselves, and spreads to our children, and to our community and on from there, creating an alternative option to the current dominant paradigm. Con't...

*The child should learn to recognize and gather wild foods such as green salad herbs, berries and nuts of the hedgerows, and "fool-proof" mushrooms such as puffballs and orange chanterelles, though they should not be allowed to eat such foods until parents have passed them as safe. And they should learn to gather firewood and cut turf for the home fires. - Juliette de Bairacli Levy*

***We will not wait around for our lives to begin.***
***We are creators!!!***
***We will make the world the way we want without***
***waiting for the old world to fall!***
***On the edge of society, joyfully outcast,***
***we dance.***
*- Wolfi Landstreicher*

"i like playing with plants 'cause it makes me feel joyful, that's my nickname - joyful. plants can be used for many things. one thing is you can make tea out of some herbs to use for healing. my favorite plants are roses. rose hips make a really good tea for you. and stinging nettles helps your blood. i like to gather plants from my garden. i pick sorrel, wild onions, violets, dandelions, fennel, and sage to make fairy salads. that's what's so good about plants. they're amazing, so be kind to them."

- Broccoli, Age 7(enjoys singing and dancing and can still make flowers bloom with her words)

## Social Justice: Herbal Aide

Check out this documentary created by Kimberly Andrade & Mary Blue based out of Providence, RI.

Their mission:

"Herbal Aide is a non-profit based organization founded to document, inspire and fund grassroots herbal projects/businesses that are working towards creating positive, sustainable social change. The Herbal Aide video documentary features herbalists who are using their passion for plants as a tool to support their community in health and healing and will be shown at herb conferences and schools in 2011".

Donations from the viewings will go into a grant fund to be given to Free Herbal Clinics, Herbal Disaster Relief and Herbal Health Center Funding.

Herbal Aide c/o Farmacy Herbs,

28 Cemetery St. Providence, RI, 02904

401-270-5223

herbalaide@riseup.net

http://www.facebook.com/pages/Herbal-Aide/173916462625591?ref=ts&v=wall

http://www.herbalaide.org/

*******

calendula

# *Herbal Baths* *by Jess*

Sliding into the warm water, their little bodies relax and peaceful eyes replace the teary ones. The bath filled with hand chosen herbs delights their tired bodies and gives distraction from injury, illness or sadness. Herbal baths are excellent for a variety of common childhood ailments. They are simple in preparation but overflowing with warmth and love.

Kids may be unable to sit still for an herbal compress or may feel uninterested in slathering on some healing oil. But if there is an injury or illness the caregiver can co-create a solution. It can meet the child's needs as well as fulfill the adults need to assist in healing. Herbal baths may work in this instance especially if the tub has a favorite bath toy or the caregiver reads a book while they soak.

Foot baths are useful if access to a large tub or enough water is problematic. Try one during the flu, a fever or a cold. One fall my son and I came down with the flu. He sat on the couch under blankets and put his feet into a small tub held up by a stool. If the treatment area is bigger than just the feet/ ankles such as with multiple bruises or cuts try a full tub bath. Con't...

<^<^<^<^<^
^<^<^<^<^<

**When to create an herbal bath?**
No need to have a special occasion but here are some moments to get you started:

**Cuts & scrapes or bruises* that cover a large area from fails, bike spills, berry-pickin', or in my children's case a typical day spent adventuring outside.

**Fever* that has become uncomfortable- tepid bath is best- foot soaks are also sweet here or herbal compresses on the legs. Of course fever isn't evil in and of itself but instead one of our bodies ways to balance itself and work with and through the illness. There are times though when relaxation or moderating a fever is needed. Remember to figure out what **your** personal comfort level is for home treatment and **trust your gut**!

**Stress* from a hard day at school, fight with siblings, over-tired and cranky, the modern, stimulating world, teething...

**Preparation:**
In a quart size canning jar place herbs. Loosely fill the jar about 1/3 full if using dry herbs-if using fresh add even more. You want to make this brew much stronger than a tea you'd drink. Cover with just boiling water and place on the lid. Let steep for 30 minutes to 2 hours. Strain out herbs and compost the marc. Add the liquid to the tub. Some people like to add essential oils to the bath but I prefer to avoid them as much as possible- I prefer whole herbs I can taste and see. It takes A LOT of raw herb to make even a small bottle of essential oil. Never add them straight to a bath- they can irritate the eyes, nose and other sensitive areas.
(For more e.o. thoughts:
http://www.massagetherapy.com/articles/index.php?article_id=567)

**Which herbs?**
This will of course vary greatly on your purpose, your kid and what you have on hand. Think about how to best match what is presenting itself to you and how different herbs act, feel and relate to the body. Use your senses- practice & tune into the plants and your child. If the ailment is hot, red and irritated-look to cooling herbs...is the wound old and oozing- try a warming dry herb... Below are common plants you may already have growing nearby or dried in your cupboard.

**Cuts, abrasions, stings and bites:** plantain, calendula, self-heal, rose petal, chamomile, violet leaves, yarrow, thyme, bee balm, or chickweed.

**Muscle strain, sprains or bruising:** yarrow, goldenrod, St. John's wort, comfrey, or elder berry

**Fever:** Elder flower is a safe yet effective, slightly sedative remedy for a child whose fever is uncomfortable. Elder flower gently assists in normalizing heat so the child can rest. For restlessness, aches and pains try catnip, linden, ginger or lemon balm.

**Flu:** For flu with intermittent chills & heat chamomile, yarrow, & linden are remedies to try. Linden and chamomile both work well when irritable or nervous. Yarrow is helpful if the flu was sudden in onset.

**Cold or Cough:** Herbs can help ease tension and loosen congestion. The possibility of herbs here is immense-try to suit them to how your child looks and feels as well as the type of cough (dry?, lots of mucous?, infection present?). Highly aromatic herbs such as some mint family (thyme, bee balm, rosemary, anise hyssop...) plants can do wonders on a congested nose and keep infection in check.

# Plantain

Story & Drawing
By Brooke Sackenheim

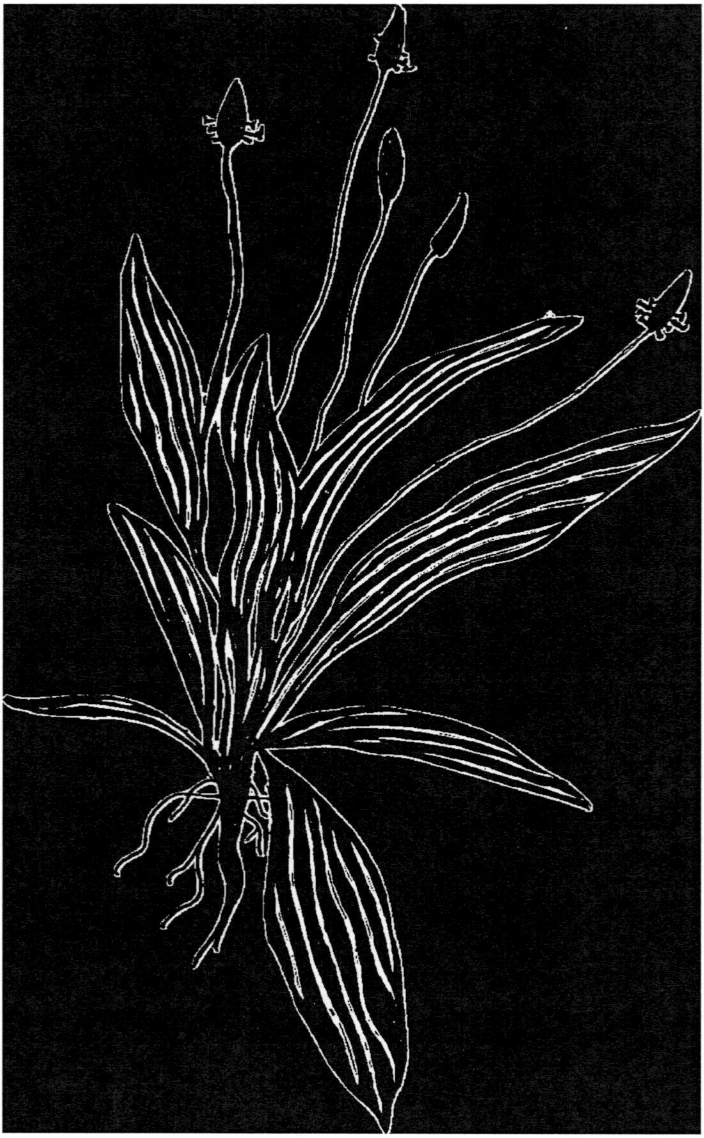

Helpful Uses of Plantain:

Cuts, Bruises, Road Rash, Hang Nails, Splinters, Burns, Stops Bleeding Wounds, Abscesses. Makes a good whistle.

When my daughter was 15 months old she was bit in the face by a dog. I didn't know what to do. When I took her to the doctor the next day, I was PANICKED. There was so much FEAR. (Would she scar? Did she need shots or stitches? Did I wait too long?)

"Dog bites are the nastiest bacterial infections." said the doctor as she gave my daughter a tetanus shot.

When I picked up the antibiotic the pharmacist told me "this medicine will smell and taste like garbage, try the best you can." I had to physically restrain my daughter while she fought and gagged the dosage down. After the second time I couldn't do it anymore. It felt WRONG. It was the OPPOSITE of healing. There had to be a better way. But I was SCARED.

I was walking through my yard, UPSET and looking down I saw 20 plants of green plantain (*Plantago lanceolata*) show themselves to me. "CHOOSE ME", they said through my body and into my head. I went inside and pulled Aviva Romm's book, Naturally Healthy Babies and Children and looked up bites. Sure enough I found remedies containing plantain and calendula. Going back outside many plants OFFERED me their leaves and each one I thanked with all of my HEART. I made tea and when presented to my child, she drank it all without complaint, every, single time. She would let me hold the poultices to her face. She HEALED.

Now 3 1/2 years later, the three tiny scars on her face are part of her character. She asks for "girl tea" and talks to plants. She is starting to know them by name. Now, I study herbs more seriously then I once did. Plantain is by far my favorite sacred ally. It fulfilled my wish of amore humane way of healing.

## *'Gaia's Garden' & 'Living Landscapes'*

game review by Physick

I was thrilled to see the herbal adventure board game 'Wildcraft!' mentioned in Fireweed #1. Since we don't own a television, boardgames are an important part of our family time and 'Wildcraft!' stands alone among boardgames. Until now that is. Living Earth Games has recently created two amazing permaculture-based cooperative games: 'Gaia's Garden' and 'Living Landscapes.' 'Gaia's Garden' is a companion planting board game for 1-6 players, ages 4 and up. The game emphasizes the value of planting vegetables and herbs based on beneficial companionship. In this way they attract predator insects to eat the pests and help maintain the overall ecological balance of the garden. By learning which specific plants enjoy each others company, children will learn that the health of a plant community (just like a human community) is based on diversity and mutual aid. If pests threaten your garden bed before it's finished, players may share plant starts from the nursery. As a result, they discover that by helping others they are helping themselves and everybody wins. The actual playing surface of 'Gaia's Garden' is decorated with lovely, soft illustrations of stepping stones and flora, and is a reproduction of original water color paintings.

Additionally, the board is comprised of recycled paper and vegetable inks and breaks down into three pieces for easier storage in its organic cotton bag.

'Living Landscapes' is a garden-design card game where the player, "learns to see relationships between the elements of a landscape and our needs." The game itself is for 2-6 players and can be played on one of two levels, from 4 to 7 years or 7 to adult.

The cards themselves are divided into three categories: Elements, Functions, and Products. When properly connected the Elements will yield Products and offer other Functions. For example an Orchard (E) will yield Fruit/Nuts (P) and offer Windbreak, Firewood, etc (F). Players cooperate to use combinations of the three groups in order to design a final landscape. What I enjoyed most about playing this with my children was the creative and unique ways they saw connections between Elements; connections that I had overlooked or hadn't even considered! Like the board game, the cards are reproductions of original water color paintings and include two blank cards for you to add your own ideas.

'Gaia's Garden' and 'Living Landscapes' are two wonderful games that will help teach sustainable permaculture design while providing hours of entertainment. One of the best ways to bring together family and friends in order to create stronger bonds is through games (both outdoor and indoor). And as our society reluctantly moves towards a post-oil world, we will have to think of alternatives to the nightly ritual of gathering around the glowing screen. I envision steaming cups of herbal tea, illuminated by candles and lanterns, as we gather round to laugh and play a game. 'Gaia's Garden' and 'Living Landscapes' will be invaluable assets to such future scenarios and should be on every family's shelf.

To order, or for more information, visit:
**etsy.com/shop/lizetfrijters or**
**livingearthgames.com.au**

(Note: Although based in Australia the games arrived fairly quickly and the shipping costs were quite reasonable. Well worth every penny!)

## Bami-Ondaadiziiike Birth Doula Project:
### *A lesson in grassroots organizing* by Dana

The Bami-Ondaadiziiike Birth Doula Project was born in 2006 through a grant with the Red Cliff Community Health Center's 'Honoring Our Children Program' under the Red Cliff Band of Lake Superior Ojibwe. We are a group of professionally trained and dedicated volunteer doulas who provide physical, emotional, and mental support for pregnant people and their families in the Chequamegon Bay area, located in northern WI.

The project is a 100% volunteer based organization. One of our primary fundraisers includes growing, making and selling herbal teas for the childbearing years. We have networked with the Red Cliff Mino-bimaadiziiwin Gitigaaning (community garden) to incorporate a birth garden, where we will be able to grow many of our own herbs. We have been grateful to have the guidance and wisdom of elders in this community as we move forward.

We would love to network with other doulas, Mamas, Papas and children who have experience with supporting families in their birth and parenting journeys. Our website is **www.goodbirth.com** and we can be reached via our referral line: 715-331-9337

Project drawing by Cait Irwin

*≈Moonwise and Prodigal Gardens≈* by Jess

I live in a region with many wonderful down to earth herbal teachers. In this issue I will show some love to two such people. Thank you to Linda Conroy and the late Rose Barlow for sharing your herbal goodness with myself and so many others. Here is a sampling of their work and please do visit their websites for more recipes and articles.

**Linda Conroy**
**http://www.moonwiseherbs.com/**

Purslane Pesto (*Portulaca oleracea*)

*This is one of my favorites. I love the flavor of this pesto. It is slightly sour, like sorrel but has a creamy texture. It is delicious served with fish or anyplace else pesto is called for.*

2 cups purslane chopped
1-1/2 cups olive oil
3 cloves garlic (or to taste)
salt (a large pinch)
Grated Cheese to taste (optional)
Nuts (a large handful and/or to taste) (optional)

Combine all of the above (except the olive oil) in a blender or food processor. Start blending and add the olive oil slowly-checking for the consistency that you prefer. If you have the option drizzle the olive oil as you blend. Pesto can be eaten fresh and/or frozen for later use. Enjoy!!

Rose Barlow
Rose passed away in June of 2009.
She remains a beloved member of her community, thank you Rose.
http://www.rosesprodigalgarden.org/

## Spring Salad

*Spring flowers add a special beauty and charm to this salad, the recipe is endlessly adaptable to whatever is available on your foraging expedition. This is a recipe I like to use on my wild food walks.*

3 cups Chickweed
3 cups grated carrots (4 or 5 medium carrots)
Add any of the following:
*Watercress
*Violet leaves and flowers
*small Dandelion leaves and flower petals
*chopped Wild Leeks
Toss everything together. Sprinkle with Violet flowers and Dandelion petals.

## Creamy Chickweed Dressing

*This recipe is truly yummy (and healthy)!*

½ cup olive oil
1 Tbsp lemon juice (or vinegar)
1 tsp honey
2 cups fresh Chickweed greens
¼ tsp salt
1 garlic clove
dash of pepper
½ cup yogurt

1. In blender or food processor, blend all ingredients but the yogurt thoroughly.
2. Add yogurt, and blend gently until smooth.

# JUNIPER

by Monica Furlong
Reviewed by Moonwolf (age 12)

'Juniper' is Monica Furlong's prequel to 'Wise Child' - reviewed in Fireweed #1. The only child of King Mark of Cornwall, Juniper is taken under the wing of her grandmother Euny. Euny is an old, wise woman who teachers her herbal lore, healing arts, and even magic.

Later, after Juniper returns home, she realizes the true meaning of her magical education; Meroot, Juniper's power-hungry aunt, is using black magic to lay waste to the crops and harm Juniper's as-yet-unborn brother.

Gamel, Juniper's childhood sweetheart, is the son of Meroot herself. But staying on the side of good he and Juniper battle together against strange curses and evil transformations, and through secret tunnels to stop Meroot, save the village, and bring peace to the land once more...An enchanting story!

marshmallow

## ♥Holistic support for the new mama in a scrubbled up world♥

### By traci picard

When a person becomes a mama for the first or 3rd or 9th time there is a special kind of change going on, and it's intense, it's never easy and most of the rituals we have relied on since the dawn of time are either gone or cheapened into oblivion. As many of you know it is difficult enough in our current addled society to keep yourself from lying in the road and waiting to be run over without the added burdens and joys of parenthood. However, the transition can be eased with a little bit of perspective; wonderful herbs and a few other healthy (groan...) life choices. I won't lie, you won't spin coal into gold but you may be able to work a lesser alchemy and manufacture a shiny nickel.

In the first few weeks your life has been turned upside down. Your identity is replaced, your body up heaved. But I am not going to address the many wonderful ways herbs can help the physical healing process. I am more concerned with the moment all the excitement wears off and you are left with a big ol' wtf that seems to stretch out in front of you for the next few years or so. The newness has worn off, your body is a new kinda normal and the world looks very very different...

The world can feel like a hostile place. The coping mechanisms you used to rely on may not work so well now. Many wonderful people succumb to depression, inertia, passing to fit in, constant tension and confusion. However! You are now part of the ancient cycle of mamas living out the process. You're doing it! And there ARE ways to increase your chance of making it through postpartum not just intact but stronger, awesomer, fiercer. Ok, maybe you won't be intact-you may lose something in the process but you will gain too-you trade in your old heart for a bigger more beautiful one which just may need a little extra protection from the cruel world.

I have compiled a list of flexible suggestions to help you make it through the day, the week, the 18 plus years...

* **Process**- the birth experience can be transformative and traumatic at the same time. Whether your birth was transcendent and awesome or painful and stressful-or a little of both-the benefits of talking about it, writing, using art, movement or sound to process and come through the whole experience can be very healing. Do it alone or with a trusted person and start yourself towards understanding what the heck happened!

* **Instincts**- post partum is a fine time to admire the way we have still got a certain special something in this techno-peopled world that is kinda magical. Sure, parents magazine and the entire medical industry deny it but mama you've got an awesome instinct inside you that has burst out-make friends with yourself. Con't...

* **Communication-** you may not even know exactly what you need. But no one else does either! Now is the time to advocate for yourself. Speak up, communicate your needs and wants to others. Family, partner(s), coworkers, health professionals, random people on the bus.... Practice now, as you will advocate for your child(ren) for years-and eventually need to teach them how to communicate!

* **Community-** having a connection with others is especially important when going through this transition. All ages! This includes other kids, elders, and everyone in between. Finding your community can be a lifelong process with ups and downs. But trusted people who have your back and you have theirs, who can be called upon in times of need or times of joy are vital to life and sanity. Cultivate your relationships like a gilded garden.

* **Daily movement-** make it a priority to get some kind of physical activity. This is not a you're-fat-lose-weight-guilt-inducer!! Moving about helps stave off the enemy of emotional wellness-stagnation. What this will look like varies greatly for different people. Some like a gentle walk, others hit the gym and yoga can be a nice option too. Try not to get hung up on your ideal-a tai chi video with a toddler "helping" or a walk with baby in the sling is way better for my morale than lying around remembering the fun stuff done before mamahood. You have a new standard now, and Movement is great for your circulation and is a time to think, get centered, and burn off some of that nervous energy.

* **Nutrition-** delicious nutritious foods help you recover physically and mentally. Especially when breastfeeding you can improve your energy level and stress load with a diet high in good protein and fiber and low in simple carbs and white sugar. Don't beat yourself up over an occasional lunch of fried clams with a shot of whiskey but aim for good meals and snacks which make you feel awesome. Processed foods can get out of the way to make room for a more nourishing approach. A good multi-vitamin can go a long way towards filling in the spaces in your culinary life and a daily dropper of liquid vitamin B can literally work wonders on the brain!

* **Projects-** a life's mission may sound daunting right now. However, having projects which you love to do, work that is meaningful, education that works for you or any kind of life practice affirms your self worth. I understand that this is hard, especially for those of us without the luxury of a wage earning partner or reasonable cash flow. However, goals power the moment in a way that nothing else can.

* **Avoid triggers-** got a questionable uncle? Fox news? Competitive and creepy mommy and me clubs? Run! You don't need to only hang with cheery fembots but those persons who make you feel like crap, question your parenting, put you down or make you feel defensive have no place in your postpartum life. And try not to spend much time facebooking with your childless semi- friends who don't understand or respect the leaky boob, the family bed or just how bad you really need a nap. Con't...

* **Sexuality**- post parenthood sexuality is a loaded topic which deserves attention. Yes you can have great sex again-but it takes more. More planning, more lube, more of a sense of humor! Of course sex may not mean intercourse-just taking time with yourself or a partner to explore your new body can help. Enjoying physical closeness with a trusted friend, self love, a little erotica can all remind you of what gets you sexually invigorated. It is easy to fall into the trap of believing people cannot be parents and sexual beings at the same time-and this is reinforced by society and the media. However you acquire it, an orgasm can be a great healing tool and connection for the body and mind. Allow me to recommend a great book! Check out The Mother's Guide to Sex by Anne Semans and Cathy Winks. Lots of relevant info for the new mama and the old mama alike!

* **Nature**- the plants are there for you. If you can get yourself out there the birds and soil and worms and water can be profoundly healing. To me, even a vacant lot of mugwort and pigeons restores my faith in the natural world. Look how the earth renews! And you will too. We can take the earth's advice and grow where we're planted. Tenacity, community, the cycles of life and a natural flow are all outside our door when we get out of the house and explore. A sense of stagnation creeps in all too easily when we spend too much time indoors. Inertia is a powerful force indeed, and a self-fulfilling kinda force.

* Oh, yeah-what about HERBS?!? Above all else, nourish. Give your body what it needs to heal, to work hard rebuilding, lactating, hauling that sweet little baby around and dealing with sleep deprivation. *Nettle, oatstraw, fennel seed, tulsi,* & *raspberry leaf* all work in an infusion. Digestion and assimilation can always use a little help-try *burdock root* and *bitters*.

Relaxation takes on a new importance-baths! With or without the baby you can steep your tired bones in *lavender* and *mint, rose, sage, cinnamon* or *vanilla*-- whatever moves you. Don't have a tub? Footbath! Follow with a massage oil-infuse herbs in a carrier oil or add a tiny bit of essential oils. Don't forget to give yourself a little of the mamalove you shower on your little one.

For tension and stress *skullcap* tincture soothes the edges. It is a very multi-purpose herb, gentle yet effective for tension headaches too. Sometimes you need to diffuse the sense of dread that creeps into your day. Also try any combination of *passion flower, milky oats, rose petals, catnip* and *chamomile* in a child-safe tincture blend. *Lemon balm* helps to restore the sense of humor/levity when it's been hijacked by life. For more severe tension a little bit of *blue vervain* can soothe jagged emotional edges well. Each person is different and an herbalist can help to come up with the right nervines for the individual.

The range of experiences we experience after becoming a mother is vast. Sometimes it feels like way too much! And that won't go away-it will ease, it will fade, it will improve but your heart has a new chamber lady and you're in for a hilly ride. A fabulous heartbreak. And you are definitely not alone.

## 'I'm a Medicine Woman, Too!'
by Jesse Wolf Hardin
Reviewed by Physick

One of my favorite children's books of all time has been Thomas J. Elpel's 'Shanleya's Quest.' In this book Elpel has taken his unique approach to plant identification (the ubiquitous 'Botany in a Day') and simplified it to help children learn basic plant families through an engaging story. Perhaps the greatest aspect of 'Shanleya's Quest' is the fact that the main character is a strong, intelligent female who bravely explores uncharted territory. 'Shanleya's Quest' raised the bar for the literature that is necessary if we are to create a new culture. To craft a book of similar quality was always going to be very tough endeavor, but Jesse Wolf Hardin accomplishes just that with 'I'm a Medicine Woman Too!'

Like 'Shanleya's Quest,' IMWT! also has a strong young female as it's protagonist. In this case it is Rhiannon, an eight year old who desires to be a Medicine Woman, but is frustrated by her young age and perceived lack of knowledge. The story is laid out in the form of a dialogue between Rhiannon and her father, who is also the narrator.

The story begins by recounting her early years spent scaling the cliffs and canyons of the Southwest, following the tracks of her animal relations, and accompanying her mother on wildcrafting excursions. As her father explains to her, it is precisely this early immersion in wilderness which laid out the foundations of her hidden knowledge.

\\\\\\\\\\

"A Medicine Woman is not something you wait to become," he points out, "it's what you do with your life, starting right now!" Her father goes on to help her see her own beauty and ability and it is here that IMWT!'s strength lies; Rhiannon is not talked down to and told of her ability, but rather she is encouraged to look within to discover for herself. This leads to IMWT! being a very empowering book for young children, which is needed now more than ever. Hardin also manages to avoid the urban/rural divide that many parents have wrestled with over time, when he describes that the Medicine Woman tradition of ancient times can still be found, "...in the trees, in the yard, or the shadowy far ends of a neighborhood park." This will effectively help children who live among concrete and power lines to feel included and encouraged to explore their own urban surrounding for edible and medicinal plants. Along the way, we meet other Medicine Women of various cultures; from the Apache reservation, a Mexican curandera, and a folk healer from the Ozark mountains. These individuals help remedy the stereotype that Herbalism is either a New Age trend or an antiquated European practice.

In the end, Rhiannon learns that everything a Medicine Woman needs - such as Compassion, Truth, and Curiosity - is already present within her, and that no matter what she does with her life, whether she becomes a farmer, artist, or teacher her unique abilities and skills will be a blessing. Con't...

Kids can take this powerful lesson with them as they go out into the world to save, defend, heal, and nurture the Earth and all her relations.

Throughout IMWT! readers will meet their plant allies both within the text ("...climbing high into a mullberry tree, gathering leaves for a lung tonic and berries for a pie") as well as the drawings (every page has Herbal and botanical illustrations incorporated into the picture). Like the story itself, the illustrations of IMWT! were also done by Hardin. Children will find these soft, colorful hand-drawn sketches calming and pleasant to the eye. Also, Hardin has included many items which parents and children will find familiar such as the excellent Wildcraft! board game lying by Rhiannon's bare feet, or the bookshelf with titles like 'Where the Wild Things Are,' Rosemary Gladstar's 'A Family Herbal' and Juliette de Bairacli Levy's 'Nature's Children.' This helps to reinforce the connection between the reader and Rhiannon.

As a bonus, at the end of the book there is a Name the Herb Game where readers can test their memory and Herbal knowledge. Example: "Page 32 - The plant and root below this Medicine Woman is a kind of wild licorice used for the lungs by Herbalists in China and elsewhere. Another classic lung Herb is the tall plant growing next to her, with soft fuzzy leaves and a tall seed stalk. What is its name?"

'I'm a Medicine Woman, Too!' is a beautiful work of art. A truly magical story that is essential if we are to realize our wildest dreams of a more healthy and beautiful world.

red raspberry

# GENERATIONS

by Terry-Anya Hayes

Most of my friends, as I grew up, were tall and leafy: the plum tree planted the day I was born; the Norway maple at the foot of our hill; a particular gnarly apple tree into which I climbed to dream, or plan, or cry. Three cedars thrust into space from the cliff beyond our house, then reached for the sun, creating perfect, child-sized saddles. I have never felt more secure or more loved than when riding above that sheer drop, or felt a loss more profound than when arguments and pleading failed and the old spruce that shaded our sun porch was cut down. Throughout my uneasy childhood and adolescence on the Maine coast, the arms of the trees were always open, a haven from the frequent turmoil at home and a living model of peace, beauty, and strength.

In my early twenties, in the heart of New York City, vowing to avoid the mistakes of my mismatched parents, I became a single mother by choice. Yet, other than loving my children unconditionally, I hadn't the foggiest idea of what I *should* do for them. I looked forward to passing along my knowledge of plants as food and medicine, but although my daughters enjoyed our herbal teas, organic vegetables, and occasional wild foods, they showed little interest in gathering or growing or befriending them. Prospect Park with its acres of linden, oak, and beech, its mulberries and June berries, was in their view just a green frame surrounding the playground, a border for the place where fun happened. So much of who I am was formed by my friendship with trees; how would my daughters fare without finding their own strong relationship with nature? Remembering that my mother, too, had lacked any evidence of hunter-gatherer genes, I swallowed my disappointment and we blundered through.

Ah, but my grandchildren! When my first granddaughter turned five, we hiked together every weekend of the summer, often with New York City's own Wildman, Steve Brill. Soon Kyana's favorite foods were steamed baby jewelweed, burdock petioles (blanched in two changes of water and lightly buttered), and the bloom stalks of cattails. When her Junior Ranger walk leader told a boy that the fragrant white flower he held was probably not toxic, Kyana took issue: "Actually," she informed the group, "Star-of-Bethlehem will make you sick." A few years later her younger brother, unwilling to spend an entire day on foot, proved himself worth his weight in mushrooms on our first short walk together. Pointing to a disreputable-looking growth at the base of a maple tree, Iiamn asked, "Is that one, Grandma?" And so we collected *Fistulina hepatica,* an uncommon, pleasantly sour, edible species that looks like liver and - in defiance of all logic - the longer you cook it, the more it resembles raw meat. Con't...

Children live closer to the ground. Their eyes are less clouded by what they expect to see. On a trip to the Prospect Park Zoo, my youngest granddaughter, Kylah, listened intently to the grownups talk about morels, those flavorful, highly-sought fungi that may or may not appear around dying elms or in orchards at apple-blossom time. Suddenly she stopped and pointed to the side of the path. With no elm or apple tree in sight, she had found the only morel I've ever seen in Prospect Park.

When Kylah was three, she began accompanying me to my new favorite hunting ground in New Jersey. We boarded a train at Penn Station, hopped off at a commuter parking lot at South Mountain Reservation, and - on weekdays, at least - had an entire mountain, with its deer and bunnies, black walnuts and berries and fungi, virtually to ourselves. And how she loved the trees, especially large, obstructive, recently fallen ones! She would fling her little body onto and over their thick trunks as if crossing into another dimension. If she began to tire before I was ready to head home, I would squint into the distance. "Kylah," I'd say, "is that a tree across the path down there?" And off she'd go, revived. I shared her love of the fallen, since that's where many mushroom species choose to grow. Sixteen years later, Kylah still tells the story of her grandmother's charge up a steep ridge to harvest a *Gymnopilus spectabilis* - the closest thing the Northeast has to a hallucinogenic mushroom - from a crumbling log. Big Laughing Gym in hand, I turned, waved, lost my balance and - in her words - cartwheeled down in slow motion, preceded by the fungus. "What did you like best about those days?" I asked her recently. She thought for a moment. "Spending time with you," she said, and a moment later added, "Knowing the names of things, even when we weren't together. I remember the first time I saw Burdock and knew its name."

Precious times for me as well. My grandchildren thrived on the lessons my children were not ready to receive. Yet today, in my grown daughters, seeds I thought had withered are alive and well: the food on their plates is fresh, local, and real; they tend to their minor ills with tinctures of Echinacea, Spilanthes, and St. John's Wort. And while Cleo, Anneke, and Cameille have few specific memories of interacting with plants (pokeberry painting aside), each tells me that the teas and fresh foods of her childhood made her feel loved and secure. *Loved and secure* - the exact feelings that suffused my gangly thirteen-year old self, dreaming on a gray limb in a cloud of apple blossoms. That sustained me at age ten as I rode my trusty cedar across the abyss. Who am I to dictate the path by which these assurances reach us? If my daughters open to the plants, their children will teach them.

## *More Suggested Books for Kids*

(for the first installment, see Fireweed #1)
Compiled by Physick

Adventures of Sheldon, the Mushroom - Tuck
Berries, Nuts, and Seeds - Burns
Crinkleroot's Guide (series) - Arnosky

Fairy Dusters and Blazing Stars - Samson
Giving Tree - Silverstein
Good Mushrooms, Bad Toadstools - Fowler

Henry Works - Johnson
Herbal Fairytales (series) - Burns
Herbs Coloring Book - Bernath

I'm a Medicine Woman, Too - Hardin
Katya's Book of Mushrooms - Arnold
Keepers of Life - Caduto

Last Wild Witch - Starhawk
Linnea in Monet's Garden - Bjork
Medicinal Plants Coloring Book - Arbel

Midwife's Apprentice - Cushman
Mushroom Hunt - Frazer
Native Plant Stories - Bruchac

Rosy's Garden - Ichikawa
Summer Witches - Tomlinson
Weslandia - Fleischman

Wildflowers - Busch
Wildflowers, Blooms, and Blossoms - Burns
Wise Woman and Her Secret - Merriam

## ♥♥♥♥Contributors Bios:♥♥♥♥

**Brooke Sackenheim** has always been in love with plants and has fond childhood memories of lying in a field of green grass with daisy chain crowns and dandelion rings. She received her first intensive herbal education in Portland, OR in 2002. An avid reader and fan of zines, she has great affection for Hot Pantz and credits it as an inspiration. Brooke is currently enrolled in Aviva Romm's program Herbal Medicine for Women. She lives in Columbus, OH with her husband, daughter, two cats and a dog.

**Dori Midnight** teaches magic and folk healing to kids and adults and maintains a healing practice committed to accessible, community healing. After 13 years of living in San Francisco, Dori recently moved to the woods of Western Massachusettes, where she is continuing her healing work, teaching, and writing.
A video about magical arts class:
**www.vimeo.com/14101311**
**Contact: www.dorilandia.com**
**Www.midnightapothecary.blogspot.com**

**Dana** is the mama of two lil' boys of 3 years and 10 months. She is honored to work with families in their childbearing years in the Chequamegon Bay (WI) area as a doula, lactation consultant and childbirth educator. She can be reached at
**northwoodsdoula@riseup.net**

Herbalist and wild foods educator **Terry-Anya Hayes** was born in Tennessee and grew up in Maine. She is an award-winning poet who writes frequently on health issues. Poetry, plants, reverence for the earth, and the desire to heal have always been part of her life. She teaches ethical wildcrafting and plant and mushroom identification wherever the herbs and fungi beckon, and leads popular classes on wild foods, herbal medicine-making, and managing health with common foods and medicinal mushrooms. She is a past president of the New York Mycological Society.

**Monkeypants** is a single mama of baby Grae in Green Bay WI. She spends her time knitting small toys and clothes for everybody that wants them. She enjoys riding bikes with a baby trailer and looking at pictures of adoptable dogs on the internet. She loves to cook vegan food and draw herbs for Fireweed.

**Kiva Rose**
I am a traditional herbalist and medicine woman, and my practice is focused on a vitalist approach to local plants, sustainability, whole person/whole plant understandings and earthy, practical ways of teaching people to work with the plants themselves rather than being dependent on experts.
**Contact: www.bearmedicineherbals.com**

**Leah Wolfe,** MPH, is a community herbalist and health educator with a background in health research and health advocacy. She teaches as a way to contribute to decentralized sources of health care, which are integral to a sustainable, ethical, and affordable system of health that emphasizes public health and autonomy. She apprenticed as a healer and studied herbal medicine at the Elderberry School of Botanical Medicine, and is certified as a Wilderness First Responder. She offers consultations and herbal medicines on a sliding-scale or gift exchange basis to make treatments accessible. She founded the Serpentine Project in 2009 to restores habitat for at-risk medicinal plants and cultivates other important medicinalplants at the Plowshares Land Trust in Wisconsin and BLD Farm in Ohio.
**Contact:**
**info@serpentine-project.org**
**www.serpentine-project.org**
**www.etsy.com/shop/thetwistedserpent**